STEVE

FOCUS + HATE fUP

CAMERON

MEETINGS SUCK

MEETINGS
SUCK

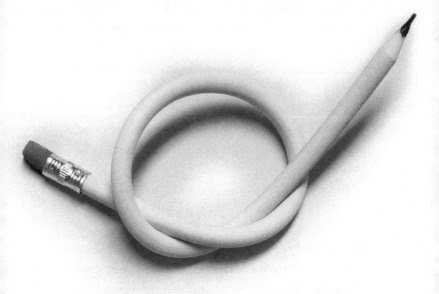

TURNING ONE OF THE MOST
LOATHED ELEMENTS OF BUSINESS INTO
ONE OF THE MOST VALUABLE

CAMERON HEROLD

"Provocative yet caring, visionary yet results-oriented, Cameron is today's CEO whisperer."

– RICH KARLGAARD, PUBLISHER, *FORBES MAGAZINE*

"Cameron has a unique ability to transform the broken into the brilliant. He does it with businesses and now he's doing it with meetings."

– SIMON SINEK, NYT BESTSELLING AUTHOR OF *START WITH WHY*

"Cameron's framework for organizing and running meetings has allowed us to get twice as much done in half the time."

– JJ VIRGIN, NYT BESTSELLING AUTHOR OF *THE VIRGIN DIET*

"Time is money and meetings are either effective or become time "black holes" dreaded by all. Cameron's practical and succinct guidelines have not only ensured our meetings yield alignment and actions, they do so with an eye toward company results and growth. Implement these now."

– RANDY ANDERSON, COO, LISTENTRUST

"*Growing companies more than ever need to communicate effectively as they scale to stay ahead and on track. Cameron has not just summarized every "needed" meeting and their structure but also has helped us eliminate wasted meetings saving our company time to stay on task. We are a more focused and connected company by incorporating his map of rhythms and meeting needed from the top to the bottom of the organization.*"

– TONY RICCIARDI, PRESIDENT, LISTENTRUST

"*Cameron coached us for over 18 months. During this time, my company grew 83%, was listed in the Inc. 5000 for the third year. Our meeting rhythms he gave us have made the company self-multiplying. I no longer even have an office at Rhythm Engineering.*"

– REGGIE CHANDRA, PRESIDENT & CEO, RHYTHM ENGINEERING

"*Most companies are drowning with meetings that employees don't want to be in, don't add value and drain company productivity. We have implemented many of Cam's best practices and now have the right meetings with the right people at the right times. Overall, we have fewer and much more productive meetings. Everyone feels more informed and they actually look forward to our meetings as they save time and improve communication.*"

– ROBERT GLAZER, FOUNDER & MANAGING
DIRECTOR, ACCELERATION PARTNERS

"Cameron, through his strategic process and specific action steps, has helped my company transform meeting into milestones. We no longer waste time or energy and our team is more energized and effective. And energy and effectiveness equal profits."

"No Agenda, no attenda! Agendas better have times for each topic so everyone knows how long we will discuss each item to use best of our time. Sounds like an easy concept but VAST majority of meetings don't have agendas and people show up and have no idea why or what they are discussing and half the time is spent going over agenda. Cameron's systems have really helped us in our rapid growth."

"Cameron's content in Meetings Suck taught us that the senior person in the room (usually me) should speak last. And using his Post-It Note exercises, most of my ideas are already on the wall. He taught me that my job is to make sure that the meetings are being run in a shorter amount of time, that they're on point, and then get out of their way so they can execute on it."

"I haven't been able to come even close to putting into words how impactful seeing your daily huddle has been for my companies. Our customers talk about how impressed they are with the organization and teamwork they see as they work with our teams. Meetings done right have been a key to creating a self-managing self-multiplying company."

— DAVID BERG, FOUNDER, REDIRECT HEALTH

"As a tenured executive of a Fortune 100 Company, I am fortunate to have Cameron as my executive coach. His entrepreneurial approach has forced me to think out of the box and approach leadership differently. He challenges me every session to plan and prepare differently for every meeting I attend or host to ensure that we continue to move our growth/turnaround agenda forward."

— JAIME JONES, PRESIDENT, SOUTH AREA, SPRINT

MEETINGS SUCK

*Turning One of the Most Loathed Elements
of Business Into One of the Most Valuable*

ISBN   978-1-61961-414-7   *Hardcover*

        978-1-61961-415-4   *Paperback*

        978-1-61961-416-1   *Ebook*

LIONCREST
PUBLISHING

To Kim, thank you for pushing me to write more books.
To Aidan, Connor, Hannah and Emily, thank you
for your patience with all the work I do.

CONTENTS

IT'S NOT THE MEETINGS...IT'S US!

"A *meeting is an event where minutes are taken and hours wasted.*"

– CAPT. JAMES T. KIRK, STAR TREK

WHEN WAS THE LAST TIME you left a meeting feeling inspired and thinking, "That was an awesome meeting!"? Or better yet, when was the last time you watched other people in the room leave inspired and saying, "That was an awesome meeting!"?

Was it yesterday? Last week? Last month? Last year?

Or maybe, never.

Sadly, it's far more likely that you've walked out of most meetings thinking, "What a waste of my time."

But I have a secret to share with you...your meetings don't have to suck.

In fact, if done right, your meetings hold the potential to drive alignment within the business; give direction; generate energy, focus, and creativity; and inspire your people to elevate the business to the next level. But when a meeting is run poorly, which happens often, then none of that is possible.

Instead what you get is a team that hates and dreads attending meetings. They find them boring; no one pays attention as they're distracted checking iPhones and responding to emails; they're lost in their mental to-do list that's a mile long and are seething that the meeting is preventing them from whittling it down; and they're confused about the purpose of the meeting and what's being discussed.

And you know what? Those, and many others, are all real and legitimate reasons to hate meetings.

Except the problem isn't that meetings suck; it's that

we suck at running them.

We aren't training or equipping our people with the right skills and tools to run effective meetings. It's like sending your kid into a Little League game without ever giving him a glove and playing catch in the backyard or teaching him how to swing a bat, how to slide into second base to avoid a tag, or even the basic rules of how to play the game. Throwing your child into a game without any preparation will only lead to an embarrassment of errors and his hatred for the experience.

And yet, that's essentially what we do with our employees when we send them into meetings without training them. Too often, business leaders complain that their teams hate meetings, while failing to look in the mirror and ask, why? And the answer is that the onus falls on the leaders to teach the employees how to run and participate in a meeting.

Otherwise, it's like a parent blaming the game of baseball for why their child hates Little League. It's not the game of baseball that's to blame; it's the parent. And the same idea applies to business meetings.

ARE MEETINGS REALLY NECESSARY?

The short answer: yes. As much as we detest meetings, they aren't going away. We spend about 20 percent our time in meetings—one-on-one meetings, coaching meetings, problem-solving meetings, brainstorming meetings, strategy meetings, and, of course, meetings that don't really require our participation.

"Why don't I eliminate all meetings?" I often hear from business leaders. Many people believe that, with our modern methods of communication such as email, we no longer need video conferencing or in-person meetings. Sure, you could replace meetings entirely with emails and nonverbal communication, but that would be a big mistake, disastrous even for the success of your business.

While email is a helpful technology, it can't replace the power of face-to-face communication. Written communication is a minefield of misunderstandings. Consider the sentence, "I didn't say you were beautiful." You can interpret that six ways depending on which word you emphasize! Six words, six different meanings—and matters only get murkier with more complexity.

Something happens during face-to face-communication that is critical to the future success of our teams and businesses. Meetings allow us to hear from people who aren't always heard; they enable us to quickly solve problems that can't be done via back-and-forth email exchanges and to build trust within our teams. Something happens to the connection among the team when you see one another across a table or over video. You hear the inflection and tone in someone's voice. You see others' facial expressions and body language. All of this helps to form deeper bonds of collaboration.

You need this group dynamic for your business to grow, so why not learn how to run and participant in meetings properly? Why not fix the problems and make your meetings matter?

Plus, it makes financial sense when you consider the cost of running a typical hour-long meeting. If you have 10 employees who each make $70,000 a year—$35 an hour, in other words—that's $350 for a one-hour meeting. In fact, the average meeting costs about $500 to $1,000 an hour.

When our meetings aren't run properly, it's a waste of money.

We can do better.

WHAT TO EXPECT FROM THIS BOOK

At some point, all of us have to run or participate in a meeting. This book is for *everyone,* from the CEO, to managers, to entrepreneurs, to frontline employees just starting their careers. Regardless of the stage of your career or your role in the company, this book will teach and give you the tools you need to run focused, time-effective meetings to help you, your teams, and your companies soar. And yes, even if you find yourself on the lower rungs of a company, you can have a tremendous impact on the meetings you attend. You too can derive great value out of meetings, while using them as opportunities to "lead up" and advance your career.

In the following pages, I will give you the easy-to-implement tools to run high-impact meetings so you can avoid wasting time, money, and resources. The book is broken into four parts. Part One deals with the unavoidable truth: meetings will happen; it's inevitable. This section teaches you how to get the most out of a meeting, regardless of your title, stage of career, personality, style, or role in the organization. The second part includes the core fundamental principles of how to run a successful meeting across all organizations, regardless of the size of your company or the meeting. The third section explains the core types of meetings every company needs and the different components. For example, regardless of size or industry, all companies need to have meetings on finance, strategy, coaching, problem-solving, and more. Finally, the fourth part of the book covers virtual meetings and how to use technology to enhance the experience.

I've had the honor of teaching and coaching hundreds of leaders—from one of the Big 4 wireless carriers to entrepreneurs to a monarch!—on how to grow their companies exponentially. For me, there is nothing more rewarding than watching my clients achieve their ultimate outcomes (profits and revenues), renew their culture, improve the atmosphere of their organization, and foster a culture that's energized, focused, and accountable.

Time and time again, I've watched how a properly run meeting enhances and strengthens the successful pursuit of leaders' goals.

Interestingly, I've coached and spoken at numerous events in twenty-eight countries, and despite the huge differences in cultures, they all have one thing in common: they conduct meetings in the same manner that we do in North America. I have an upcoming trip to Qatar to coach the Sheikh. I've never been and know very little about the country. And although there are vast differences between their culture and my own, they're looking for the same structural model for how to run a meeting that we use in North America and Japan in our businesses.

That's because, when done right, it works.

I'm sharing the lessons with which I coach my clients with you in this book, because if you learn more about meetings, you will become a more effective leader, manager, or participant. Again, regardless of your position, the tools in these pages can help you to grow your career.

Plus, I want you to walk out of a meeting smiling, feeling inspired, and thinking, "That was awesome! Let's get to work!" Too many people leave the office feeling as if they provided no value to the organization during the day. I want to flip that feeling for you. After reading this book, you will know the model for running effective, powerful, and valuable meetings. And when you use this model, not only will your meetings improve, but you will imbue them with renewed focus, energy, and accountability—elements that will also help to improve and drive your company culture.

The day has come to elevate your meetings and your role in them, and to use meetings as a tool to take your company and your career to the next level.

We have work to do—let's get started.

PART ONE

AT SOME POINT WE WILL ALL RUN A MEETING

———

This section of the book is about addressing why meetings matter. It's about taking stock of your situation, your current landscape at work, and looking at what value you're getting or not getting from meetings. At some point, each of us will probably have to run our own meeting. So if you always complain about everybody else's meetings, wouldn't it be a great time to learn how to run them properly so you do a killer job at it?

KEY CONCEPTS

BEFORE DIVING INTO the crux of this book, it's important for me to introduce a few key principles and concepts to you that you will find in the coming chapters. First, whether you attend or run a meeting, you have to impact it in a positive, meaningful way. It's about more than walking into the room and sitting quietly at the table while the meeting happens around you. No, it requires you to have a give-and-take approach where you gain value from being present, and you give value by speaking up. This means you need to become comfortable raising your ideas, even if those ideas conflict with others in the room.

AGENDAS

Another key principle is the agenda. This is a must-have to understand the flow of a meeting, to stay on topic, and to save time. It's up to each attendee to know how to spend his or her time, how to give value, and how to leave the meeting feeling it was worthwhile. Truthfully, if you or your people attend a meeting that wastes your time, or if you aren't providing value, then it's better to have skipped, called in sick, or stayed at your desks finishing your work.

You can save a significant amount of time by having a proper agenda and allowing your people to opt in or out of meetings to which they don't feel they can add value. It's kind of like special teams in football. The placekicker, for instance, isn't stepping onto the field every down, but he has to be there for the plays when he's needed. So too, a frontline employee doesn't necessarily need to be at every meeting. He or she may have other more important and impactful things to work on.

For this efficiency to work, though, people need the opportunity to "lead up," which means a frontline employee must be able to push back on a manager and say, "Why are we going to a meeting for which we don't know what is on the agenda?" or "Can you fill out the agenda more so I know which parts I should come to and which ones I can perhaps opt out of?" or "I read through the agenda, and I don't really need to be here for that. I think there are a couple of others who don't need to be here either."

Regardless of rank, people need the freedom and permission to raise their hands during a meeting to say, "I disagree," or "I think differently." And they must know their opinion will be heard—in fact, regardless of position, everyone on your team deserves to be heard. Everyone in a meeting should be considered equals.

TYPES OF MEETINGS

A variety of meeting types exist, about which I will go into greater detail in Part Three. So as not to overwhelm you when we get to those chapters, here I will give you a brief explanation of each meeting type. As I walk you through the important steps to running a successful meeting in the following chapters, I encourage you to imagine using one of the meetings below as a key visual and example.

YEARLY AND QUARTERLY RETREATS

This type of meeting is essential for leadership teams. These meetings ensure alignment, strengthen team building, and promote skill development. These meetings always happen off-site, preferably in a comfortable, relaxed environment surrounded by nature and away from external distractions.

QUARTERLY BOARD OF ADVISORS MEETINGS

The purpose of this meeting is to discuss how the company will achieve desired growth. This is an opportunity to review the vision for the next three years (what I call the Vivid Vision, which you can read about in chapter 9), financial statements, and compare where the business currently stands with where it's intended to be.

MONTHLY FINANCIAL MEETINGS

These meetings get your team on the same financial page. Here, employees will have the opportunity to review the company's income statement, obsess over how to make more money, and find savings. These meetings not only provide a level of transparency that makes everyone feel secure, but they teach your team valuable lessons about finance.

WEEKLY ACTION REVIEW OR WAR MEETINGS

The WAR meeting is a ninety-minute meeting that

each business area holds for its team. The purpose is for the team members to update one another about what they're working on and to keep everyone on the same page. It forces people to hold one another accountable, while allowing for teammates to share experiences and to help each other out of challenging situations. These meetings build and unify teams and help to prevent divisions.

WEEKLY STRATEGY MEETINGS

These are meetings in which the leadership team discusses opportunities six months to a year out. The meetings help to build a strong strategic mindset within the company. They also ensure that the team has time to manage this area of the business, which often is overlooked due to their managing urgent day-to-day matters. These meetings can also be held on a semi-monthly basis, if every week is too much.

WEEKLY GOAL-SETTING AND REVIEW MEETINGS

These meetings, otherwise known as the One-on-One, occur between a leader and a person who directly reports to that leader. In my experience, this is the most consequential type of meeting because it allows the leader to set goals for the upcoming week and to establish a rhythm and focus for team members.

These meetings help motivate and inspire, and simultaneously, they provide employees with the support system and necessary tools they need to create change.

DAILY HUDDLES AND ADRENALINE MEETINGS *Line Up.*

Daily huddles are seven-minute, all-company, energy-boosting sessions held during the lull times of the day (typically around 11:00 a.m. and 2:00 p.m.) that keep your team pumped and inspired. The first couple of minutes involve good news. Anyone is allowed to share good news or praise employees, customers, leaders, and so on.

Next is the numbers portion of the meeting, which involves posting key metrics so that everyone is aware of where things stand—for example, sharing sales figures. Team members can compare these metrics with expectations and goals. Then the team leader provides a daily forecast, measuring monthly and yearly revenues against the budget. This is not just a list of what the numbers *are*, but more importantly, what numbers *mean*. This helps to show the team members the value of their contribution to the company.

After sharing the numbers, the team leader dives into development. This is when the members rotate, with each business area updating the entire company. This brings everyone up to speed on how each area of the company is doing, including their top three items for the quarter and what's in store for the coming week. This systematically guarantees that business areas remain focused on their quarterly goals.

Next up is the missing systems and frustrations portion. This is an opportunity to share potential hazards in a no-blame environment. This is not the time or place in which the problem is debated or resolved; instead, this is when someone volunteers to take initiative to see that the problem is addressed.

Finally, the meeting ends on a high note with the high-gloss cheer. The cheer is based on the good news from the day's huddle and allows for everyone to stand and unite as a team.

For companies under about twenty people—a huge slice of the market—everyone in the company could read aloud his or her top three priorities for the day. This generates connection among the team. When a company grows beyond twenty employees, however, this becomes information overload.

The Adrenaline Meeting is an outgrowth of the huddle for businesses that have expanded to the point that a huddle is too large. Adrenaline Meetings last three to five minutes and are held by the individual business areas, rather than company-wide. Ideally, these meetings serve as pre-huddle meetings, getting everyone on the team up to speed with what everyone is working on that day. These meetings operate with the same format as the huddle, but in this case, each person within the meeting is usually given the opportunity to speak.

AD HOC DEBRIEF MEETINGS

These are quick five- to ten-minute informal meetings that allow the team who ran a project, call, or event to debrief others on how it went. These are booked on an ad hoc basis as time permits. However, you should schedule these meetings shortly after the project is complete, so that it is still fresh in people's minds. This type of meeting is helpful in uncovering the things that went right—and wrong—with the project, with an eye to improving things for next time.

CEOS, MANAGERS, AND EMPLOYEES

COMPANIES HAVE THREE TIERS or types of employees: (1) leaders, which includes CEOS and C-suite
executives; (2) middle managers, which includes
midlevel managers and executives, and (3) people
on the front line, like your sales force. Each of these
tiers has different needs and goals that they want to
achieve in their meetings.

HIERARCHY OVERVIEW

Leaders—the CEO, other C-suite officers, executives—have profit-and-loss responsibilities with
three resources at their disposal to achieve their

goals: people, time, and money. They apply these resources as carefully as if they were held at gunpoint, so as to ensure that everything is spent wisely and nothing is wasted. If their people attend meetings without adding or receiving any value, then they've wasted their three resources. In fact, if we multiply the number of days, weeks, and months in a year that someone spends in a meeting, then the business could face a loss of up to 20 percent of that person's salary because of time spent in useless meetings.

The goal of middle managers is to move up in the organization, so they're trying to grow as leaders. One way to accomplish this is to show they're effective at leveraging the resources they have access to. The better they run meetings, the more they will accomplish. The more they accomplish, the more they will push forward. The more they push forward, the more output they will generate from their resources. The more output they generate from their resources, the more they will showcase their leadership abilities—and their potential to climb the ranks in the organization.

For frontline staff, it's good to go into meetings recognizing the chance to stand out among their peers. Especially within larger organizations, it's easy to feel like a number and to blend into the crowd. The meeting can be a fish bowl, or a stage, for their career. It can show they're dialed in or buttoned up. It can show they're respectful or unable to listen and work with people. The meeting is their chance to show they can "lead up" in the organization. Really, it's their chance to show their stuff to the people that can help their career trajectory.

I realize it may seem a little political to go into a meeting thinking of your own agenda, but at the end of the day, you should treat a meeting like a job interview. You wouldn't go into a job interview without being prepared. You wouldn't go into a job interview late. You wouldn't go into a job interview without putting your best foot forward.

If you treat the meeting like a job interview, you will stand out in front of your peers, leaders, and those who directly report to you. Not to mention that the meeting is a great place where people can leave work at the end of the day thinking, "Wow, the eight or ten hours I spent at work were all valuable today," rather than walking out demoralized and thinking, "Wow, a third of my time was wasted in meetings...again."

HOW THE HIERARCHY IS RELEVANT IN MEETINGS

If everyone is equal in the room, then why do hierarchies matter?

First, during the meeting the most senior person, or the person booking it, has to think of themselves as the CEO. Why? Well, as I explained before, CEOs have profit-and-loss responsibilities with three resources to wield: people, time, and money. CEOs think and act in terms of maximizing these resources to create value. As the CEO, you wouldn't want to waste your people's time in a meeting, because that loses you money and resources. This is the same mindset that the senior leader who is running the meeting needs to adopt. Preferably, I'd love to see everyone in the room, from the frontline team member to senior management, embrace this thinking, because it focuses your attention on how to create the most value.

Here's an example. Say Bob's time is worth fifty dollars an hour. Would you burn up a fifty-dollar bill? Of course not—if Bob's coming to the meeting, you want to ensure you get fifty dollars worth of value from him. Otherwise, you're better off having him do something other than attend the meeting. This is true for every person that attends a meeting. If it's happening on your time, it's happening on your dime. CEOs live this motto, and by adopting the CEO mindset, you will place yourself in a position to adopt this philosophy too.

The second reason a hierarchy still applies is that part

of the CEO's job is to grow the next crop of leaders. They don't want to tell their people what to do all the time. They want to grow and develop them as problem-solvers, as thinkers, as strategists, and as tacticians. They want to teach them not to fear conflict, so they can have good, healthy debates that lead to better decisions and more growth for the company.

Whoever is leading the meeting needs to keep this lesson in mind, just as all participants need to remember that meetings provide an ideal opportunity to grow their skillset as future leaders.

There's another crucial reason to grow future leaders, one that's practical and makes common sense. When subordinates can successfully manage meetings, then CEOs, their C-suite officers, and other leaders in the company will have the time and freedom to focus on higher-level initiatives. This is crucial. Time and freedom to hone in on the highest-priority tasks isn't a mere luxury; it's a necessity if a business is to expand and fulfill its potential.

As CEO, one of the things I've found to be extremely useful in helping people grow is my speaking less. As I will discuss in the next chapter, different personality types manifest in meetings. Some people are more vocal, while others remain quiet. But just because people are quiet doesn't mean they don't have ideas. In fact, they do. If you can create a format where everyone can speak and share their ideas, then the vocal people will likely hear their own and new ideas coming from those quiet sources. In fact, when I spoke less in meetings, I often heard my ideas pitched by others.

If you raise the skill level of your people, you will raise their confidence. But their confidence will never grow unless they're able to raise a good idea and have others engage with it. When an idea is accepted by the team, then the person who raised it will begin to feel confident to raise more ideas. This is exactly what you and the company needs.

For example, let's say I'm the CEO, and you're part of my frontline staff. We have the same idea about where to go for dinner: a Mexican restaurant. Well, if I suggest it, you'd say something like, "Yeah, I was thinking the same thing." But it doesn't make you feel good, because you didn't say it first. But if you suggest Mexican, and I respond, "That's a great idea. I was thinking the same thing," all of a sudden, you're thinking, "Wow, he liked my idea," and you feel a burst of confidence. Now, you're more likely to raise other, bigger ideas in the future.

As the CEO, it's not important to share your ideas; it's important to drive the company in the direction you want to go. The best way to do that is to develop leaders—people who can think critically, who are comfortable sharing their ideas, and who engage in debates. And as you will learn in Part Two—particularly the chapters on communication, roles, and styles—meetings lose all value when you run them like a power trip. In fact, they need to be the opposite.

INTROVERTS AND EXTROVERTS

DURING A MEETING, you will encounter four types of personality traits: Dominant, Expressive, Analytical, and Amiable. Everyone, including you, has a primary and secondary trait. Understanding the different personalities, and your own, will help you to better manage and engage with everyone during a meeting.

PERSONALITIES OVERVIEW

Diagram 1 is a four-box matrix that shows which personalities will emerge during a meeting. In the top left corner are the **Dominant** types. These individuals are extroverts, assertive, verbose, forceful, strong, type-A, and driven personalities. They will say what they mean, argue for it, and act forcefully. They believe so strongly in their opinions that they will push for them. Often, these people will argue for the sake of being right rather than for having the better solution.

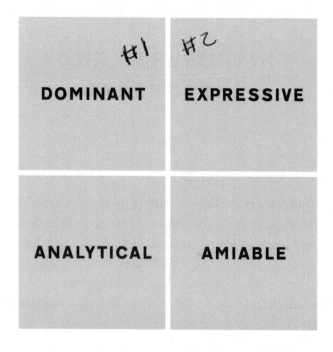

In the top right corner, you have the **Expressive** types. These individuals are also extroverts, plus they are animated, talk with their hands, and think out loud. They tend to get excitable and emotional, and they eagerly jump in to speak.

Analytical people will literally think through their answers before speaking and tend to be introverts. Typically they think through their answers for so long that Dominant and Expressive people feel they're too slow, or not really thinking. This doesn't mean that Analytical people don't have the right answers; it means they have a different thinking process.

Often, the Dominant and Expressive personalities in a group appear to wing their remarks, or shoot from the hip. But it's not really shooting from the hip, but instead thinking out loud. These types need to say seven things out loud before arriving at their final answer. The Analyticals, by comparison, do their thinking in their heads. When they speak up, they've already gone through the seven possible answers internally, so the answer they share is their final one.

And finally, on the bottom right of the diagram, you have the **Amiable** personality. These individuals avoid conflict and tend to get along in a passive manner. Amiables will say things like, "Well, whatever," or "Whatever you'd like," or "That's fine," or "I'm okay too." Truthfully, they mean it most of the time. However, when they walk away, they often feel as if no one really cared how they feel. Or they will leave a meeting thinking they didn't add value or didn't have anything to say, or no one asked them anything, so they should have stayed at their desks. Sometimes these personalities can be passive-aggressive, but more often passive.

Of the four types, Amiables have the hardest time getting their ideas heard and embraced. And there's some truth to their feelings and the thoughts they commonly have when they leave a meeting. But wouldn't it be great if we did hear them and even once in a while took their ideas into account? Because if we don't care about their ideas or want to listen to what they say, or if they're not going to speak, then why are they coming to the meeting?

Generally speaking, Analyticals and Amiables often work in fields such as IT, finance, or communications, while Dominants and Expressives tend to work in sales, marketing, and public relations.

PERSONALITIES IN MEETINGS

When you're leading or participating in a meeting, the biggest challenge is preventing the Dominants and Expressives from steamrolling the Analyticals and Amiables. This isn't necessarily a negative thing, because when you run a meeting, you can rest assured knowing these people will engage and speak out. However, you do have to worry about them not hearing others, taking over the meeting, or not caring about the agenda. Most of the time, they need simple reassurance that they've been heard, their ideas captured, and their contributions understood. The great thing about these individuals is they accept that being heard doesn't mean the leader will always take their ideas.

If your meeting does get overtaken by the Dominants and Expressives, then the problem is that most Analyticals and Amiables will keep their ideas to themselves or, if they do speak out, be ignored.

An instance from my own life may help illustrate what can happen when this dilemma arises.

When I worked as the COO of a company, the CEO and I were both very Dominant and very Expressive. Meanwhile, we had a vice president of finance who was probably Amiable as a primary trait and Analytical as a secondary trait. He was very quiet, soft-spoken, and polite. He regularly told us to be careful and that he worried about our numbers.

"I'm worried about the spending," he'd say, and then he'd highlight other potentially fatal flaws in the organization that he foresaw.

"Yeah, yeah. But here's why it works," the CEO and I would reply. Then we'd sell him on our ideas while we plowed over his objections. Because we were so domineering and forward-driving as Dominants and Expressives, we refused to hear him tell us that there was a problem. When suddenly a new CFO came into the company and announced, "We're running out of money," we were shocked to learn this.

All we could think was, why were we just learning about this now? Then, we realized we *did* know about it. We had just ignored it. It was like driving down the highway and seeing a sign that says, "Caution: Bridge Out," but trying to convince ourselves that we could make it work. But there was no bridge, and we almost lost the company over our inability to hear what was being said over our own voices and ideas.

To avoid a situation like mine, I encourage you to identify your personality types. Understand their strengths and weaknesses so you can address some of the natural pitfalls and mistakes.

My primary trait is Expressive and my secondary is Dominant. I talk with my hands and think out loud. I'm very emotional and take things extremely personally. I've had to develop a number of tactics to balance myself and to ensure I don't overwhelm my colleagues. For one, I've learned to sit on my hands, which I know sounds weird, but it works because it prevents me from starting to talk.

Another tactic is to count my ideas on my fingers. I will hold my finger out to remind myself that I have an idea, but that I can wait to say it instead of jumping into the conversation immediately. I will also make an attempt to listen to the person speaking, and maybe I will ask a question or two to understand their point before sharing mine.

Finally, I'm cognizant to ask the youngest person or newest member of the group to speak first and share their ideas before I give mine to the group.

Once you identify your type, you too can start developing your own tactics to address some of the issues you might face in a meeting. The ones I described above can work for Dominants and Expressives.

Analyticals and Amiables should begin by realizing their worth and value. If you've been invited to the meeting, that means people believe you will add value. Your task is to ask yourself, "How can I best provide value?" It's probably by sharing ideas and information, so understanding that your thoughts are wanted will make you more likely to offer them. Then, try and make a conscious effort to speak at least once during a meeting or to write down your ideas.

EVERY BOX OF THE ORGANIZATION CHART

BECAUSE ALL CORNERS of your company can benefit from the vehicle of meetings, you need to consider all corners of your company when you're inviting people to participate. From IT to human resources, from marketing to public relations, from finance to sales, every department has vital information that can help the team make better decisions.

The best way to describe this is to imagine you work for a theater company that's about to put on a stage production of *The Phantom of the Opera*. It takes about two hundred people to pull off a show. Besides the director, producer, and actors, you have people selling tickets, creating marketing campaigns, handling the lighting, making the costumes, producing set designs, selling food at concession stands, and ushering people to their seats. Only a handful of people make it on stage, but without them, you'd never have the other 195 people working behind the scenes. And without the 195 people working behind the scenes, you'd never have those five people on stage.

Just like the play, your organization needs every single person for the show to go on. And while all employees are necessary for the organization to run and grow, not all of them are needed to be on stage—or in this case, at a meeting. Too often, organizations invite everybody on the payroll to a meeting instead of the most essential people. You might have a dozen people able to add value to a meeting, but if you can get it covered with five, then cover it with five. The trick is carefully to select people from key departments with particular expertise and skills that can provide value and insight during the meeting.

Another way to look at this is in the way the Navy Seals conduct field missions. My job on the mission is to look left, your job is to look right, Charlie's job is to focus straight ahead, and Steve's job is to look behind. But if I were to look anywhere but left, then I would put all of our lives at risk. I need to trust that you and the rest of our team is doing the job they were assigned, and you need to trust that I'm doing mine. In any mission, the Seals don't send more men than necessary, nor do they send too few. Each person on the team is there because he provides value. And there's an expectation that accompanies everyone on a mission: that they will do their job right. The same concept holds in a meeting.

TO INCLUDE OR NOT TO INCLUDE FRONTLINE STAFF

The frontline staff have a vital perspective to offer in a meeting, because they're the ones dealing directly with customers on a day-to-day basis. Often, higher-ups have less insight into this external perspective, which leads to a blind spot.

Therefore, the frontline staff quite often have value to add to a meeting. Unfortunately, proper training and setting expectations is required for frontline staff to provide this invaluable insight. The initial reaction of many frontline staff invited to a meeting is, "Oh God, I'm going to another meeting." In fact, frontline staff should feel the opposite. They should think, "Wow, I got invited to this meeting! This means they want me to add value. How can I best add value?" and "I'm being invited to this meeting, which means I should be able to leave with value. What value can I extract and leave with?"

Frontline staff should walk into every meeting with these two purposes—to add value and to receive value—in mind.

As I said earlier, these meetings also serve as an opportunity to help frontline staff grow as leaders, so they can move up the ranks in the organization. If frontline staff sit there checking their phones, disengaged, rolling their eyes, and not adding or receiving value, then they're better off working at their desks.

Again, if you're organizing a meeting and inviting someone to attend, it's because you see value *for* them or you need value *from* them. This means you have to create an environment for them to give and receive that value. Otherwise, leave them out of the meeting. It's a poor use of money, time, and people.

ALL DEPARTMENTS BENEFIT FROM MEETINGS

Let's assume that your organizational chart has ten functional areas, such as marketing, IT, finance, sales, customer service, engineering, and public relations to name a few. All of these departments will hold their own meetings, as well as participate in meetings hosted by others.

Let's take a look at some of the different types of

meetings these departments likely will hold.

Marketing. This department will hold meetings on strategy, creative briefings, and budgeting.

IT. The IT department will have functional requirement meetings and integration meetings. They're also likely to participate in meetings with other departments that are considering tying IT into their work and projects. For example, if marketing has an IT need, then IT representatives will need to be on hand during the marketing team's budget and resourcing discussions.

Finance. Some of this department's meetings will include budgeting and strategy, which relates to spending money and use of cash. Often, this team is involved in hiring decisions, which impacts other departments and human resources.

Sales. Meetings for this team include budgeting, strategy on how to close sales, and training sessions on how to grow as salespeople.

Customer service. This team often discusses strategy. The team works closely with leadership to let them know what's happening in the field. Their feedback explains to leadership what is or isn't going well with the company's products or services. They will closely work on problem-solving with the leadership branch. Customer service might also be involved with IT integration or engineering meetings.

Engineering. This team is necessary for product development, application support, and operations. They will also be involved in hiring and firing, strategy, and competition meetings.

Public Relations. This team is likely to work closely with the marketing and sales departments, and they may be involved with engineering for recruiting support.

In the end, no matter your role or which department you work in, I guarantee you will participate in meetings. The question is whether you will take advantage of the opportunities to provide and extract value, or if you will let those chances slip by.

PART TWO

HOW TO RUN A SUCCESSFUL MEETING

—

This section of the book outlines five specific, proven strategies for taking back and maintaining control of your company meetings, both large and small.

PREPARING AN AGENDA

WITHOUT QUESTION, every meeting must have a clear agenda distributed to attendees in advance. If you skip creating an agenda, then your meetings can quickly go off track, get hijacked by a random topic, or include people who shouldn't be attending. I've found that without an agenda guiding the discussion, it's also common for attendees to ramble, engage in simultaneous side-conversations, or devolve into catcalling—all outcomes detrimental to taking your company to the next level.

However, by taking the time to plan, prepare, and distribute an agenda before the meeting, you will reap considerable benefits.

THE FOUR BENEFITS OF AGENDAS

BENEFIT 1: INTROVERTS ARE ENGAGED

When it comes to your more introverted team members—Analyticals and Amiables—more often than not, they won't speak up unless you ask them a question directly or they're passionate and engaged in the subject. Giving them an agenda in advance allows them the time they need to think through answers, frame their thoughts, write them down, prepare a statement, or whatever else they need to do to raise their ideas. If an agenda is not given to these individuals ahead of time, you will likely lose great ideas that will remain unspoken and will walk out of the room with them when the meeting is finished.

BENEFIT 2: TIME IS MAXIMIZED

Creating an agenda in advance gives you the distinct advantage of maximizing your time. When you include how long each item is up for discussion, this helps you realize whether you've allocated too much or too little time for certain subjects. This gives you flexibility to adjust and split topics into separate groups before the meeting begins, instead of trying to navigate this on the fly.

You can also save time in the beginning of the meeting

by skipping an introduction in which you cover what will be addressed. By giving attendees the agenda in advance, you can immediately dive into the discussion the moment the meeting begins. Plus, if an agenda item is scheduled for three minutes and you know the next one is for fifteen minutes, then you can control your time, the flow of ideas, and communication more efficiently.

BENEFIT 3: ONLY ESSENTIAL EMPLOYEES PARTICIPATE

Creating your agenda in advance forces you to think critically about who you're inviting. Often I see leaders show up for a meeting only to realize they've invited too many people or the wrong ones. I firmly believe it's vital only to invite individuals for the portion of the agenda for which they're needed.

When you're creating your agenda, it's helpful to ask two questions about attendees:

1. Do I need to have all these people I'm thinking about inviting?

2. Do these people need to sit through the entire meeting, or do I only need them for a portion of the meeting, on a particular subject?

I mentioned this earlier, but imagine that everyone who shows up represents fifty dollars. It doesn't sound like a lot, but if you invite the wrong two people, or two people come to an unnecessary meeting every day, then you've wasted one hundred dollars and prevented two people from providing more value by remaining at their desks and getting their work done. Say this happens once a day; that's one hundred dollars a day, multiplied by 250 operating days. That is $25,000 a year that disappeared because you invited the wrong people to a meeting. If this goes on for years, then it could cost your company hundreds of thousands of dollars. And that's only if you're inviting two people wrongly. Imagine if the majority of people attending meetings in the company shouldn't be?

One of the best ideas I've heard on the subject of resource-saving comes from Amazon.com founder Jeff Bezos, who said he would never hold a meeting in which two pizzas couldn't feed the entire group. That's brilliant. If you go beyond the two pizza max as you build your agenda, then you know to split the meeting into separate ones.

It's also highly likely that only select individuals need to discuss certain items on the agenda. That's okay. I like to think of each of these people like the sniper who waits for hours, sometimes all day, until he's told to shoot his target. If you think he's not doing anything during that time, you're wrong. Although his role is to pull a trigger, he knows he only gets one chance to make the shot.

It's the same for people brought into a meeting to provide one area of value. Sometimes you won't need people to participate for the entire meeting. When this occurs, your invitation to them can be: "Come in. Give us four data points, and then you're free to leave," or "Come in and listen to what we're thinking, and tell us if it can be done." Maybe it's an IT guy who needs to say yes or no to one question, but who doesn't need to be present for the larger discussion.

BENEFIT 4: PEOPLE LEARN TO OPT OUT

Providing an agenda before the meeting makes people feel like there's a good reason for them to attend. But giving people the agenda before the meeting also gives people the chance to opt out if they don't feel they can provide or extract value. This is a great skill to teach people, because you want them to evaluate and decide how best they can serve and provide value to the organization.

If they see the agenda before the meeting, it gives them the chance to say, "Well, there's a bunch of stuff here, but I have no ideas, don't really care, or don't think I will get or receive any value."

But sometimes opting out isn't all or nothing; people may come for either the entire meeting or none of it. When you send out the agenda, topics, and the duration for each item, then people can look at it and say, "Hey, there's an hour's worth of time allocated, and we're covering seven topics. It looks like only items three and four are valuable, so I will just show up for those points." Or they can say, "I will come at the beginning, but I will leave right after item four, skipping items five, six, and seven so I can get back and do my other work."

When people make these choices, we should cheer them for their decision to stay focused on their responsibilities and priorities instead of becoming involved in everything. They're looking through the lens of how best to generate value for the company through their time and resources, and this is exactly what we want to encourage all our people to do.

Plus, when people opt out who don't believe they can provide value, then only those who do believe they can provide value will sit around the table to engage in a more focused discussion.

While I say to celebrate those individuals who choose to opt out, I also wish to give a quick word of caution. Although it's often the right decision, opting out requires a delicate touch. You need to explain your reason for choosing to skip a meeting. Maintaining a tone of respect is crucial for your career.

Here's an example of what a respectful reply to a meeting invitation would look like: "While I would love to be in this meeting, I don't feel that I have anything specific to add. Unless you truly want me there, I have three other projects I would rather dedicate our company's time to."

Bear in mind that choosing to opt out may be a political misstep. If it's the only time you get in front of the CEO or other senior leaders, then you should choose to opt out infrequently. But if you're the person who only shows up at critical meetings and who provides tremendous value, then selectively opting out could be the better career move for you. In this instance, you're the one completing your projects instead of sitting in meetings you shouldn't be.

Finally, opting out also applies to the CEO and other senior leaders. Why show up to a meeting when your team is perfectly capable of handling it? Unless you can provide or receive value, you too should hit the opt-out button. Not only will you feel liberated and free to focus your energy on other priorities, but your team will feel empowered by your trust and faith in them to get the job done right.

BENEFIT 5: YOUR TEAM COMES PREPARED

When you include the meeting style (information sharing, creative discussion, or consensus decision) in the agenda, then you tell your team what to expect and how best to prepare. These three styles define the format of any meeting, whether it's on strategy, finance, operations, coaching, or another topic. I go into these styles in greater detail in the next chapter, but here's a quick overview of what these styles mean:

Giving the meeting style to your team ahead of time is a crucial piece of information, because then they will know whether they need to listen, offer ideas, or debate the merits of a decision on a given agenda item. They get frustrated when they are uncertain how to act. If they don't know what they're supposed to do on each subject, then they might wonder what is happening. For example, if they don't know it is an information sharing session, they might be confused about why a topic wasn't open for discussion. Or in a creative discussion, they may sit and question why a decision isn't being made.

Prep for Strategic Planning Offsite

■ Cameron Herold ∨

Add Location

Monday, Apr 4   10:30 AM to 11:30 AM

Add Invitees

Purpose: Have Full Agenda for Strategic Planning Meeting Finalized

Outcomes:
1) Finalize food ideas
2) Finalize Roles & Agenda
3) Discuss hiring an outside facilitator

Agenda:
-10 min - Discuss & Decide on rough food options, so EA can finalize
-20 min - Finalize Agenda for both days
-10 min - Discuss hiring facilitator - pros & cons

Diagram 2 shows an actual calendar invite, with a meeting request that includes an agenda, purpose, and outcome.

"No agenda, no attenda" is my motto. This is mandatory. If I don't receive an agenda, I won't go to a meeting, and neither should you or your employees. Keep your agenda simple, short, and sweet. It should be so brief that it could be written on a Post-It Note. You don't need reams and reams of content—people don't have the time for it. Use normal black-and-white colors, and skip the fancy fonts. Include a bulleted list of action items to be discussed in the order they will be addressed, the time allotted for each topic, and the meeting style chosen.

I'm asked a lot about handing out hard copies. Personally, I dislike them and feel they're unnecessary. However, some people like to distribute hard copies in the meeting because they prefer that employees engage on paper instead of on a device that could potentially distract them with nonmeeting-related material. There's no hard or fast rule, but find what works for you or adhere to what your meeting organizer prefers.

On your agenda, you will also want to include two other key components: the purpose and possible outcomes.

The purpose of the meeting is one sentence included on the agenda that tells people exactly why they're asked to attend. Then you should lay out up to three possible outcomes for the meeting. I suggest one purpose and three outcomes, because if you attempt to cover more, too many people get invited on too many tangential topics, and time is wasted. This is a way to keep meetings shorter to maximize efficiency and provide greater impact.

Imagine a family of five watching Dad pack the car for a trip for an hour. They aren't doing anything but standing there staring at Dad. Well, aren't there better things they could do with that time? Yes, of course there are. Mom could make lunch; the kids could do homework or other chores around the house that need to be completed before they leave. It's the same principle for meetings.

When you include the agenda with all items, a purpose, and possible outcomes, then people will know exactly why they have been asked to attend the meeting and what they will be expected to accomplish during it. This will prevent your people from standing around and watching.

Recently, I've toyed with adding a fourth item to my agendas: a to-do task list. I'd include this at the bottom of the agenda. It could include a list of material to read or prep work to be done prior to the meeting. This would spur attendees to think about the meeting and the topics before they arrive, so they can show up with ideas or, if applicable, have read relevant background information in advance.

DETERMINING A MEETING STYLE

AS I MENTIONED in the previous chapter, you have three meeting styles to choose from: information sharing, creative discussion, or consensus decision. This is a big decision for the meeting leader, because it tells your team how best to prepare for each topic on the agenda. Your meeting can quickly go off the rails when someone thinks the purpose is to share information when it's really to drive to a decision. As a participant, it's also important to pay attention to the style chosen for each agenda item, so you can properly prepare and add value to the discussion.

Remember: each bulleted item on the agenda will

include one of these three styles. Hypothetically, you could engage in all three styles in one meeting. For example, one item may be a ten-minute information share, while the next is a five-minute consensus decision, followed by a fifteen-minute creative discussion, followed by another ten-minute creative discussion.

Let's examine the three styles more closely, so you can understand when and how to use them in a meeting, and how best to prepare. To illustrate these three distinct styles, imagine that one of the bulleted items on the agenda is to determine where your group will eat lunch.

INFORMATION SHARING

In this example, the leader might announce, "We're going to the Greek restaurant for lunch."

In an information sharing meeting, the information flows in one direction. That direction can flow "upward" from employees to leadership, it can flow "downward" from senior management to employees, or it can flow side to side, among employees on the same rung of the company hierarchy.

Often this style is used for weekly updates, to share new ideas, or to provide feedback.

The key with this style, though, is it's a one-way flow of information without discussion, debate, or a decision reached by the group. People should be allowed to ask questions for clarification, but this is in no way an invitation to engage in a back-and-forth conversation or dialogue. It is just the sharing of information, that's all.

One of the great benefits of this type of meeting is that it's streamlined. This style runs like a tight ship. It only becomes problematic when attendees don't realize it was going to be an information sharing meeting and come with expectations to discuss or debate issues. But that's the fault of the person organizing the meeting and is easily remedied by sending the agenda in advance and announcing the styles.

Imagine meeting about a Christmas party and the first fifteen minutes are spent with people sharing their ideas. However, the party has already been planned, the location is booked, and it's a done deal. You've not only wasted that time, but you've made people mad and unhappy.

Another pitfall to watch out for with this style is to make sure the information being shared requires an in-person meeting. It's better to resist the temptation to organize a meeting if you can accomplish the purpose through an office memo.

CREATIVE DISCUSSION

Using the example of where to eat lunch, the creative discussion style would pose a question to the group for debate, such as: "Where does everyone think we should go for lunch?"

The creative discussion style revolves around brainstorming with the goal to place lots of ideas on the table. This isn't about making a decision or debating the viability of each idea. It's about embracing possibilities.

As a leader, this style allows you to accumulate a wealth of ideas that may have previously remained unknown. And because this isn't a forum to vote or to denigrate ideas, more people, such as the Analyticals and Amiables, willingly and more readily speak out and share their opinions. This is true for anyone who feels that his or her voice doesn't carry as much weight in voting situations.

When you use this style, it's important to remind people that you chose them to attend because you believe they have value to provide. Reiterating this point helps encourage people to share all their ideas instead of holding them back.

Like information sharing, this style can cause a few

problems for your team, especially when they don't understand the nature of the meeting. When they aren't told in advance that the meeting is to share their ideas without reaching a decision, many will feel upset. Returning to the Christmas party idea, if the group is under the impression that the boss is going to announce plans for the party, but in fact the boss has no clue and is looking for their ideas, then the room is likely to feel frustrated.

Another pitfall is that many participants may constantly play devil's advocate, without a constructive end. In this instance, you will need another kind of meeting to make a decision, like the consensus decision style.

However, if you need another meeting, then it's important to let your people know this. They will become upset and frustrated if they believe the meeting is to conclude without a decision via a show of hands, or if they learn the boss intends to make a decision without them. This situation is bad for team unity.

As a leader, you can avoid the latter by explaining to your team that you will use the ideas generated to advance the company plan later. You may also want to tell them who will hear their ideas, like the Board, for example, at the next shareholder meeting.

CONSENSUS DECISION

Returning to our lunch dilemma, if the consensus decision meeting style is used, then the leader would raise a question such as, "Where does everyone think we should go for lunch?" followed by a statement such as, "We will vote on ideas until we reach a consensus."

In this style, a decision is, in fact, made by the people in the room. Ideally, this unifies people as a team, since everyone feels that they have had a hand in making the decision, even if they disagree with the final result.

However, problems can arise when people leave the meeting unhappy with the decision reached and also feel like they weren't part of the process. Again, I can't reiterate strongly enough how important it is that people understand the nature of the meeting to which they're invited to attend. If one of the bulleted items involves a consensus decision, it's critical that invitees understand that their voice is welcome and will be heard. Everyone should leave such a meeting with the relief that they spoke their piece.

I have one rule when using this style: once the meeting is over, discussion on the matter is closed. I want my people to leave the room knowing they reached the decision as a team. Quibbling in the halls chews away at that team unity.

All meeting styles have pros and cons, but miscommunication and misplaced expectations cause the cons. As the organizer of a meeting, it's incumbent upon you to communicate clearly and set the right expectations for team. And if you're attending, know what you're walking into.

STARTING ON TIME, ENDING EARLY, AND COMPRESSING TIME

IF YOU HAVE EVER WATCHED an Olympic swimming event, you know there's a pre-swim routine for athletes. They stand behind their starting blocks pumping themselves up with music blasting through their ear phones as they get into the zone, ready to compete. Then they strip down to their bathing suits, stretch a little, and take a few deep breaths. The announcer calls them to their places, and they get into their ready positions. Finally, the gun fires—on time—and splash! They hit the water and the race begins.

Now, if you're a swimmer and you show up right on time—that is, when the gun fires—then you're actually late. It's true in meetings too. To be on time is to arrive five minutes early. For Hall of Fame coach Vince Lombardi, if you weren't fifteen minutes early, you were late.

THE PHILOSOPHY OF BEING ON TIME

Punctuality is not so much a virtue, which suggests it's in some way above and beyond what's required. Rather, it reflects a larger philosophy of showing respect. "Sorry, I'm late" translates in business as "Screw you, I don't respect you."

Like the Olympic swimmer, it's impossible to perform at a high level if you arrive when the gun goes off—that is, when the meeting starts. You can also glean a lot about a company simply by judging its level of promptness. For instance, how can you expect to deliver goods and services to your customers in a timely fashion if you can't start a meeting on time?

Whatever the excuse, people show up late for one reason: they haven't stopped working soon enough.

I once taught a program at the Massachusetts Institute of Technology called The Entrepreneurial Masters

Program. The class consisted of more than sixty CEOs from around the world. During class, I explained that we'd take a ten-minute break, and I'd use the stop-watch on my phone to ensure we started on time. I promised them that we'd always start on time.

At nine minutes, I took my place at the podium and waited. When ten minutes had clicked off, I went back to teaching. About one-fourth of the people in the class were still outside. I watched as they practically ran to their seats. No one attempted to apologize. They knew they'd be ridiculed for any attempt to explain away their tardiness.

There are some things that simply aren't appropriate. You wouldn't go to your grandmother's house and drop the "F bomb"; that's not okay. Tardiness isn't okay either. And it's up to you as the leader to set the expectation that being on time means showing up five minutes early and being ready to go. It's also up to you as an attendee to show your respect by sitting in your chair five minutes before the meeting starts.

The best way to be early (read: on time) is to ensure your previous engagement doesn't run late. You can accomplish this by adopting a mindset where you stop whatever you're doing five minutes early. This gives you time to go to the bathroom, grab a cup of coffee, say hi to your assistant, check emails, or grab a seat before the gun fires.

I also recommend carrying forward this concept of ending what you're working on five minutes early when you're in charge of a meeting. It's a bit unusual, but ending the meeting five minutes early gives you and your team time to transition to the next meeting or activity.

COMPRESSING TIME

Parkinson's law states, "Work expands so as to fill the time available for its completion." With that in mind, it's incumbent on us to find ways to compress time. One method is to reconsider the amount of time you initially expect you will need to achieve a task. Instead of booking a two-hour meeting, can you accomplish it in an hour with greater concentration?

"How long will it take to clean up your room?" and "How quickly can you clean up your room?" are two different questions that reflect different mindsets. The latter question compresses time and encourages you to achieve your task in less time than you think it would take. This approach and mindset is what we need to adopt when we organize meetings.

For example, let's say you want to take your team off-site for a day. But do you really need a full day? Can you compress time and accomplish your goals in half a day? If you go for half a day, then you've saved money, time, and resources and boosted your productivity. If eight people attended the off-site meeting for half a day (four hours), that's thirty-two man hours. If these eight people made fifty dollars an hour, then you've spent $1,600 for a half a day. You've also saved $1,600 by compressing the full-day meeting (which would have lasted eight hours) into four.

In general, meetings and obligations tend to fill the space you give them. Estimate how long you think a meeting, or task, will take, and then cut it in half. By limiting the time, you increase your productivity, maximize efficiency, and implement a more highly profitable system of time management.

Other useful tools to increase your efficiency include eliminating idle chatter and putting time limits on tasks during a meeting. Instead of saying, "Everyone, write down your ideas," and then waiting until they finish, say, "Everyone, you have two minutes to write down your ideas. Go."

FOSTERING USEFUL COMMUNICATION

AS I MENTIONED in chapter 2, sometimes the same people tend to speak up in every meeting. But the Dominant and Expressive personalities often forget to include the more senior people over the junior level employees.

But everyone needs to be heard during a meeting. If you don't need to hear from someone in the meeting, and that person silently sits in his or her chair, then that person didn't need to be there. You want the more silent, reserved people to speak up, because they could add tremendous value to the discussion.

HEALTHY CONFLICT

You want everyone participating, because you need a healthy dose of conflict and differing opinions. Unfortunately, conflict is a common deterrent during a discussion. People shy away from speaking up and sharing a dissenting view because it makes them uncomfortable.

But just because people disagree doesn't mean they dislike each other. Healthy conflict is the result of two people arguing passionately over what they believe is right. As long as the argument is to move an idea or agenda item forward, and not merely for the sake of being "right," conflict is healthy and should be used to advance the company.

The one caveat to conflict is when it involves senior leaders arguing in front of the group. Sometimes, alignment must be displayed among the leadership team. The group needs to see that everyone is on the same page even if differences need sorting. If that's the case, then sort those details out in a more private setting after the meeting.

ENCOURAGING ALL TO PARTICIPATE

So what should you do when you have quieter, more reserved people in a meeting? The best thing you can do as the leader is first to hold your ideas back until the end. Too often, leaders offer their ideas first. But people don't become confident, or grow as leaders, by listening to what you have to say. Instead, you need to encourage the members of the team to offer their ideas first, especially those less inclined to speak up.

Ask the quieter types—the Analyticals and the Amiables—and junior folks what they're thinking. One day, those junior members will become senior leaders and the quiet types may also be required to run meetings. The more confidence they acquire under your leadership, the better, more effective leaders they will become.

Once you've called on the junior and quieter types, then move on to the more talkative types and then the senior staff. When you solicit feedback in this way, you build people's confidence and ensure that you hear from all viewpoints. Plus, if a good idea emerges, then the team has solved the problem on its own, which builds confidence and unity too.

BANNING DEVICES?

Regarding devices, I don't see them as a problem in the same way that I don't see guns as a problem, *per se*. Both require people to act inappropriately before these things become problematic. Personally, I prefer not to use devices during a meeting. However, some people find them helpful. I know many people who take notes on a laptop. But checking email is distracting.

I subscribe to the rule that, if you're on your device, I can call you out for checking email or doing something irrelevant in the meeting. If you're guilty, then you buy the group lunch. But if I call you out and I'm wrong, then I buy everyone lunch.

Goodlife Fitness, Canada's largest fitness company, has a policy that if someone's phone goes off or if someone is caught using it for nonbusiness-related work, then everyone in the room has to do ten push-ups. Part of their core values is to be fit, so it's fun and breaks the meeting up with laughter. Plus, people learn very quickly to watch their device usage when they're the cause of coworkers having to do push-ups.

KNOWING YOUR ROLE

EVERY MEETING must include five key roles: the Moderator, the Parking Lot, the Timekeeper, the Participants, and the Closer. Each of these five roles is crucial to running successful meetings, and taking the time to assign each of the roles at the beginning of each meeting will make your meetings more efficient and effective.

If your employees aren't going to read this whole book, have them read this chapter in order to understand each of the roles and how to perform them.

THE MODERATOR

The Moderator is the chairperson of the meeting who

is tasked with ensuring that everyone stays on track, covers agenda items in the allotted time, and facilitates a quality discussion. His or her main focus during the meeting is to keep the discussion from going sideways. This requires a Moderator to be skilled at interrupting discussions and able to hurry items along when needed. It's also the Moderator's responsibility to kick off the meeting with a quick reminder about the purpose before diving into the agenda.

As I've mentioned before, the meeting is a terrific place to help people grow into leaders, and it's the task of the Moderator to accomplish this. A good Moderator will look around the room and observe which people need to engage more, and which people need to back off a bit. It's up to them to prompt the more introverted employees to share their ideas by asking insightful questions to draw them out.

And while a valuable discussion is important, the Moderator can never lose sight of the agenda or the clock. Sometimes this means he or she will need to hurry a discussion along, to end one and then move on to the next.

As the meeting closes, it's up to the Moderator to evaluate whether all the participants should attend the next meeting.

And this may sound surprising, but the Moderator doesn't have to be the one who organized the meeting. The team leader could organize the meeting, but tap someone on the team to act as the Moderator during the discussion. That's another great way to grow talent.

THE PARKING LOT

The Parking Lot person is the one who keeps the notepad of the good ideas brought up but that couldn't be addressed because they weren't on the agenda. This person will collect the ideas, so the team can return to them later, either at the end of the meeting or at a subsequent one. When the Parking Lot person hears ideas not aligned with the agenda or discussion, it's also his or her job to step in and say things like, "That's a great idea, can you guys take it offline?" or "We don't have time for that right now; can we add that to the parking lot?"

THE TIMEKEEPER

The Timekeeper's role is to ensure that each agenda item is covered in the proper order and within the time allotted. When it appears that a topic may run long, the Timekeeper will speak up to remind the group how much time remains. This is a proactive role, and the Timekeeper will watch and alert the group to any offtrack discussions before the conversation digresses. In this role, the Timekeeper isn't supposed to sit passively and wait until the clock strikes to tell the group that time is up; he or she can use an alarm clock for that.

PARTICIPANTS

Participants are the people who arrive prepared and ready to contribute for the duration of the meeting, or the part(s) of the meeting they're attending. They offer their ideas, learn valuable information, and grow as leaders. Participants should engage in healthy conflict, unafraid to argue or debate the merits of their points and ideas. They add and receive value in every meeting they attend.

THE CLOSER

Often, the Moderator will also act as the Closer. But you can also have the most senior person or the organizer of the meeting take on this role. The Closer is the person who assigns duties and timelines at the end of the meeting. He or she will summarize everything that was covered, and then go around the room to make sure everyone understands what they committed to do and the deadline to complete it.

This is important for two reasons. First, participants commit to a duty and a timeline in front of the group. This makes it nearly impossible for someone to show up at the following meeting without having done his or her work. If you hire people who deliver what they promise and who honor their commitments, then this commitment won't be a problem.

Second, clarity arises when the Closer asks people to reiterate what they've agreed to do and when. It easily happens that someone might mistake what was asked of them in the meeting. When someone says out loud that they will do a specific task, then it gives the group a chance to say, "Wait a minute. No, that was a discussion. We were just chatting about that. You don't actually need to do that." This short exercise can save people considerable time and aggravation.

Personally, I'm not a fan of the cheesy, one-word or one-sentence close where you ask the room, "How are we feeling about the meeting?" Usually people say "great" or "stupid." That's a waste of time. Save those two minutes, end your meeting early, and get back to work.

TYPES OF MEETINGS

———

Part Three is all about what specific types of meetings you need to implement and why. Above all, this section of the book will make clear that you need a system in place in order run effective meetings. You need to establish a series of regularly occurring meetings that are designed to achieve various objectives, and these meetings need to happen even when you or other members of the team are unable to attend. Canceling or postponing meetings is a slippery slope.

QUARTERLY AND YEARLY RETREATS

EVERY LEADERSHIP TEAM and business area needs yearly and quarterly off-site retreats away from the constant distractions and demands of running the day-to-day business. These retreats generate alignment, build team unity, develop skills, and encourage productive engagement.

QUARTERLY RETREATS

Ideally, your leadership team would do a quarterly retreat, and each business area would also meet on a quarterly basis.

When you meet on a quarterly basis, it's like pressing the restart button. It's your chance to review and recommit to your yearly plan. You can reassess projects and possibly reorder them, decide on new ones to start, and evaluate any ones that may encounter delays. This is when your team isolates the highest-impact projects from the big shiny objectives that can easily and quickly distract and overwhelm a company. This is your chance to sit down and look quarter by quarter at the company and match it against your Vivid Vision (which I will explain later in this chapter) to see how closely it aligns.

Often, the quarterly retreat is a full-day or half-day event that's held in the city you do business in, but outside of your office walls. Typically, I will book a suite from 8:00 a.m. to 5:00 p.m. at a local hotel. But you can book a house or a business club if you prefer. The idea is to hold the event in a single day and to go off-site to shake up the thinking of your team.

When you remove your people from their daily routines, it gives them space to think clearly and strategically about the future and what they, the team, and the company will focus on.

YEARLY RETREATS

I recommend doing a yearly retreat three months prior to the start of the next calendar or fiscal year. For example, if you run on a January through December year, you would go off-site in September or October with your leadership team. This meeting is typically a one- to two-day, or possibly two-night, session that includes skill development (like leadership, problem-solving, or coaching), team building, and planning.

I'm a big fan of hosting this meeting during the week instead of on the weekend. Weekends should be reserved for people to rejuvenate and spend time with their friends and family. The best location to hold this event, in my opinion, is in a home such as a bed-and-breakfast, cottage, summer house, or winter cabin.

Contrary to what you may think, this option doesn't have to be expensive. In fact, you could save money. If you have eight people and each hotel room costs $300 a night, then you're spending $2,400 for a one-night stay. Meanwhile, you can easily rent a large place that fits everyone for $1,500 a night through Airbnb at great locations.

When we stay in one home, I give the team a food budget and task them with shopping for supplies.

Then we divvy up cooking responsibilities with a couple people assigned to cook dinner, a couple breakfast, and a couple lunch. At the end of the day, we take a break from work, pop the cork on wine bottles, pour drinks, and turn on the music.

I got the idea to host annual retreats like this from a scene in the movie *The Big Chill*, where a group of former college friends convene for a weekend reunion at a winter house. Everyone shared in cooking dinner as they danced in the kitchen, just reconnecting and having a good time.

When your group is together and doing normal non-business-related activities, this is when the real team building starts. It doesn't happen by doing the cheesy team-building exercises with a rope and balls. It happens by hanging out, breaking bread, living, learning, and being silly together. I love doing these retreats in a shared rustic space more than doing them at a hotel where each person is alone in his or her room. There's just something special that happens from being together in one setting, living and working under one roof, and connecting outside of the office.

During these retreats, I also like to encourage leisure activities that don't require a lot of skill, such as road hockey, for which you can grab a bunch of cheap hockey sticks and plastic nets. Broom hockey works too, because it's kind of like hockey but with a broom and a ball. Kickball, played with a big rubber ball, is a good time. And instead of baseball, I opt for Whiffle ball; it's a lot less serious, and people loosen up and laugh a lot. If you're in the mountains or on a lake, you could plan a hike. When you're outdoors and breathing fresh air, you enhance and develop quality relationships among team members.

Holding a game night is another fantastic idea. However, I'd steer away from skill-based games. Play charades, Taboo, or another board game—anything that doesn't involve knowledge of trivia or a lifetime of mastery. In all these leisure activities, the idea is to keep the playing field level and your team having fun and bonding. You don't want activities that involve a lot of skill or competition. Scratch that basketball game, even if it's just three-on-three.

During the yearly retreat, you can also ask people to create a personal bucket list, or what I call "101 dream goals." Everyone lists 101 things they want to do, try, or experience or the places they want to go in life. Then together you share and talk about those dreams as a team-building exercise. Or you can take the bucket lists and decide as a group what you're going to attempt for the year. This exercise leaves people feeling excited and inspired to accomplish their dreams when they leave the retreat.

A lot of leaders wonder how much prep work should be assigned for these events. You don't have to overdo it. One of the best tactics is to assign the team chapters from a business book to read and take notes on before the retreat. Business books aren't novels, so you can select and read stand-alone chapters without difficulty. For example, you could assign your team to read and take notes on the chapter on vision from my book *Double Double* or a chapter on leadership from the book *Good to Great* by Jim Collins. Or you could read the worksheets in the back of *Five Dysfunctions of a Team* by Patrick Lencioni.

This exercise serves a dual purpose. It's team building and skill developing. It also helps your team start to think and to look into the future for planning purposes, which is a core function of the yearly retreat.

This meeting in particular is your chance to get your team to generate ideas and discuss plans about where the company is headed next year and beyond. During your time away from the office, you will look at the core goals for the year, such as revenue, profit, customer engagement, strategic initiatives, employee satisfaction, and customer satisfaction, to name a few.

Then as a team you will lean forward into the future, imagining what that future looks like, and then plan for it based on where the company is today and what actions need to be taken now.

You will want to set goals for three years out, and then do a spot analysis to look at the current strengths and weaknesses of the company, as well as the opportunities and threats you face as a team. It's like reverse engineering or bridging a gap between today and the future. You always want your team to be thinking about the future even while they plan and execute for today.

Ideally, at all annual sessions—and yes, quarterly planning sessions too—you'd review core values, purpose, and your Vivid Vision.

VIVID VISION OVERVIEW

The idea that you can throw a bunch of words on a whiteboard and mash together a sentence to describe a company's vision doesn't work. It's never worked. A Vivid Vision, on the other hand, involves a CEO leaning out into the future, almost like entering a time machine and going three years out. I wrote about this concept in my previous book, but for the purposes of this one, I will briefly explain what the Vivid Vision is.

A CEO leans into the future with the purpose of describing every aspect of the company in vivid detail, noting every area of the organization chart, listening to what the customers say, what the employees say, and what the media writes about the company. It's like standing in the future and reporting back on the details of it. This is the Vivid Vision.

What the Vivid Vision doesn't explain is how the future will unfold. It's like a homeowner who shows rough sketches to a contractor and says, "Build me this. This is my finished house." The contractor then takes the plans and draws blueprints. Then, the workers look at the blueprints and they attempt to recreate the vision. That's the purpose of the Vivid Vision. The CEO shares the vision in a general way that everyone can see and then begin to create.

It's necessary to revisit the Vivid Vision at the yearly and quarterly retreats, so that we think about the future and plan accordingly for the next quarter. Furthermore, after we've established the Vivid Vision, we must work in reverse to build a bridge to the future.

First, we look at where we want to be in three years, and then we backtrack to the step before that future in three years, and then we go back another step, and another, and another, and another until we reach where we are today. Once we reach today, then we know the step(s) we need to take to start us on our journey toward the Vivid Vision.

This may seem a simple task, but experiencing that vision of the future requires more than looking at business numbers. Most leaders discover they need a different set of skills from those they normally use in order to experience the Vivid Vision.

The Vivid Vision must be shared by everyone on the team and remain in focus at all times. If you and your team don't see the same vision of what the company will look and feel like in three years, then there's no chance the company you see in your mind's eye will ever come to pass.

VIVID VISION CHECKLIST

Pretend you traveled in a time machine three years into the future on December 31. You're walking around your company's headquarters with a clipboard in hand and a series of questions written on the paper. These questions will help you to create your Vivid Vision.

· What do you see?
· What do you hear?
· What are your clients saying?

- What is the media writing about you?
- What kind of comments are your employees making at the water cooler?
- What is the buzz about you in your community?
- What is your marketing like? Are you marketing your goods or services globally? Are you launching new online and TV ads?
- How is the company running day-to-day? Is it organized and running like a clock?
- What kind of stuff do you do every day? Are you focused on strategy, team building, customer relationships, and so on?
- What do the company's financials reveal?
- How are you funded?
- Are the core values realized among your employees? How?

Once you put the answers on paper, you can write a detailed description of all the thoughts you had generated through mind-mapping. This is what I did when I worked at 1-800-GOT-JUNK. I organized my thoughts by every department and area of the business to include marketing, public relations, sales, IT, operations, finance, production, communication, customer service, engineering, as well as values, culture, employee engagement, and work-life balance. I finished with a three-page summary that vividly described the details of the company in three years.

This Vivid Vision gives you and your team a glimpse into the future, a future for your company. It doesn't tell you how to get there, just what it looks like.

I have included a few hall-of-fame-level examples of what a Vivid Vision can look like, and I also have a copy of my own on my website: CameronHerold.com.

SNAPSHOT OF THE RETREAT

Participants: Leadership team; individual business areas

Frequency: Quarterly; yearly

Duration: Quarterly: half a day to a full day; yearly: one to two full days and possibly nights

Meeting Style: Creative discussion; consensus decision

QUARTERLY BOARD OF ADVISORS MEETING

BOARDS OF ADVISORS exist to provide advice, feedback, and accountability, and to ask thought-provoking, probing questions to push the company to new heights. Usually, I gather about five people to meet quarterly at an off-site location for four to six hours. You can also do this in an office or boardroom.

In advance of the meeting, your Board should receive a package of prep materials to read, such as financial statements, updates on what's going well and what isn't, areas where the business might be stuck, successes during the last quarter, core goals for each business area, and the company plan for the next quarter and year.

I always begin our meetings with a review of the Vivid Vision to ensure everyone is on the same page about where the company is going in three years. This also sets the stage for us to reverse engineer what we must set in motion today to get us to that future.

Every quarter, I recommend inviting one person from the company's leadership team to present to the Board. This challenges and pushes your leaders, and it's an opportunity for the Board to see what's happening at a more strategic leadership level.

The rest of the meeting is mostly related to two core goals the leadership team is focused on for the next year—not necessarily the next quarter but the next twelve to eighteen months. This could be a big strategic initiative for which you need the Board's advice, their help in troubleshooting, or their challenging questions.

It's common, and necessary, for the Board to raises the "what if" questions during these debates. They will ask tough questions, but in the end, this will strengthen your ideas and your team.

SNAPSHOT OF MEETING

Participants: CEO, Board of Advisors, plus one individual from the leadership team

Frequency: Quarterly

Duration: Four to six hours

Meeting Style: Information sharing; creative discussion

QUARTERLY BUSINESS AREA REVIEWS

MOST COMPANIES SKIP holding Quarterly Business Area Reviews at their peril. When a company reaches the apex of rapid growth, these meetings become a crucial linchpin to ensure accountability.

The Quarterly Business Area Review meeting is a half-day gathering between the executive leadership team, the heads of each business area, and sometimes the Board of Advisors. In these meetings, every business area is given about thirty minutes of airtime to provide updates. For example, the marketing team holds court for roughly thirty minutes, followed by finance, then IT, then engineering, and so on until all areas are covered.

Every business area presents using a standard template to answer questions such as these:

· What are the goals for the next quarter?
· What were the goals for the last quarter?
· Were those goals hit or missed?
· If the goals were missed, why?
· What is the plan to drive metrics and get projects accomplished in the upcoming quarter?

Each business area presents their core numbers—the metrics or benchmarks they use to measure the successful attainment of their goals. The actual numbers are measured against the goal numbers to see if they hit their target and to consider the plan to boost those numbers. These numbers give insight in determining goals for the next quarter.

Yes, this is a high-pressure meeting, with assumptions and goals challenged by the executive leadership team and other leaders. But that's a good thing, because this is when a team can address potential barriers and find ways to overcome them before disaster strikes the company.

For example, the marketing department presents its plan for the quarter. They talk about where they're headed, where they've been, their key numbers, and where they might be stuck. Then everyone in the room has a chance to ask the marketing team about their plans. The IT leader may ask, "What about this?" Then the sales leader may ask, "Have you thought about doing it this way?" Then someone from the Board of Advisors could jump in and say, "Can you move this project forward?

I love these meetings, because this is when your group starts acting as a team rather than as individuals. Everyone is engaged in all aspects of the business, and they see how important their area is in making the company stronger and more successful. Plus, when you ask select people from different areas to present in front of your leadership team, then you get the bonus of helping to nurture and grow new leaders within the company.

SNAPSHOT OF MEETING

Participants: Executive leadership team; the heads of each business area; sometimes the Board of Advisors

Frequency: Quarterly

Duration: Half a day

Meeting Style: Information sharing; creative discussion

CHAPTER 13

MONTHLY FINANCIAL MEETINGS

THE MONTHLY FINANCIAL MEETING is *the* chance to get the entire company on the same page. You want to begin these meetings by handing out copies of the Profit and Loss (P&L) financial statement to everyone in the room. You will then walk through the P&L line by line to review and discuss how the company performed.

This meeting helps people from all business areas to realize they're on the same team. And they begin to think about the company's profits and losses as if they were their own. It actively encourages them to obsess about how to make and save more money for the business.

I like to ask a series of questions designed to look at the actual numbers versus the goal. These questions include the following:

· What was our budget?
· What did we spend?
· How will we improve for next quarter?

For example, I'd take the line item for entertainment and ask the team what our budget was. Then I'd ask them to look at what we actually spent in real dollars. Finally, I'd ask how we will do better next quarter to stay within or below our budget. Once we have wrapped up the entertainment line item discussion, then I'd move on to the next one, such as the travel budget, and repeat the same questions for every line item.

By doing this in-depth review every month, you can quickly assess how successful your team is in reaching its goals and quickly change course when necessary.

ASSIGNING RESEARCH TO THE TEAM

It's best to appoint one person to be responsible for each line item at the meeting. This doesn't need to be someone on your leadership team or someone in accounting. It can be anyone within the company.

You could have one person dig into the general ledger to look at all the actual expenses and then report back at the finance meeting. One person might be responsible for telephone, another for travel, and another for office supplies. When a different person is digging into each actual expense, he or she can be specific about what happened and why. For example, one might come to the meeting and say, "We were over on entertainment, and here's three reasons why this happened." This process starts to drive the company's decision-making since it involves cutting expenses or driving revenue.

You will be amazed at some of the ideas your employees come up with. Someone in IT might have an idea for marketing, while someone in marketing might have an idea for collections.

Additionally, this process teaches your employees about a new area of the business through the P&L statement. They learn directly about how cash flow works, why certain ratios are important, how banks are involved, and how to make decisions around financing. Lots of people are curious about these items, but generally they don't raise their hands during a meeting to ask.

You also get the added bonus of helping your

leadership team to develop their skills on reading and analyzing financial statements. Often this is an area that people struggle to understand, so by walking through every line item on the P&L, you're ensuring your team builds their skills in this critical business function.

At the end of the meeting, collect the P&L statements and shred them, so you don't risk having them leaked to the public.

THE BENEFITS OF TRANSPARENCY WITHIN A COMPANY

There's much debate in the business world about how transparent a company should be to its own employees with its financials. Personally, I prefer full transparency in the business as it regards financial matters. The reality is that most employees have no idea how much money is being made. Their natural inclination is to assume, based on the company's revenue, that the CEO makes significantly more money than is typically the case.

When I was running a painting business in my early twenties, my friends who worked for me thought I made too much money. They all thought I was getting rich. The reality was that I wasn't making *any* money. But they based their assumptions on the revenue generated without understanding the expenses we paid out. They didn't understand payroll taxes, overhead, marketing costs, and the myriad other expenses that come with running a business. They only understood the revenue because that's the only number they saw.

As soon as I opened up and shared the P&L statement with them, they saw how little I made after expenses. By sharing this information, they had more insight at their fingertips and could see the big picture. In one day, they went from feeling like I was taking over the world to worrying we were going bankrupt. Their attitudes and commitments fundamentally shifted the moment I chose transparency, and we were better for it.

In another instance, I was working with a company called I Love Rewards, now called Achievers. When we went through their P&L statement as a team, we realized the company wasn't going to make its budget for the next year. There wasn't enough cash flow. This forced us to take a critical look at the sixty employees, and eventually we determined we had to cut 30 percent of the employee base. This move allowed the company to restructure, but it was only taken because the team looked at the numbers together and saw the bigger picture. All of them understood that adjustments were necessary if the company was to remain in business.

Now, normally if you made that kind of a cut to a company, you would have a revolt on your hands, but when everyone was able to look at the numbers together, the path forward declared itself. Transparency instilled the team with confidence and trust in their actions.

If you're still unconvinced about the power of transparency, here's one more story for you. Years ago, I was coaching a CEO who worried that his employees thought he was rich. Well, he was rich. At the end of the day, the employees had no idea how much money he was making, but they knew he flew around in a private jet and saw he had a limo pick him up from work each day. He was living a completely different lifestyle than they were.

I told him, "They know you're wealthy. Why don't you open up the financial statements and show them what's really going on? Give them an opportunity to learn about financials. Teach them about personal cash flow and about budgeting."

He decided to put a program in place to teach everyone how financial statements worked. Suddenly, his employees came to respect that he had created his wealth. They felt inspired in their own lives too because he was going to try to teach them the business. His willingness to open up and become transparent became an incredibly powerful thing for his employees.

He had never wanted them to see where he lived. I advised him to bring them over to his place. As soon as he did, they saw what he had, and it actually wasn't as big a barrier as either side had imagined. He was no longer hiding his wealth as if it was a dirty secret that they must never know. As a result, his employees changed their mindset.

People often ask, "Do you really want all the employees to know what everybody makes?" Sure. After all, if the workplace is a meritocracy and you want everyone on the team to do their best, why would you worry about showing off the rewards for their achievements?

All public companies show the various pay levels for each position. They show what the company and the leadership team pockets. We shouldn't be as embarrassed about that stuff as we are. What we need to do is teach people how the financials really work. They need to understand that we don't take the entire profit home at the end of the day and roll around in it. Taxes consume about a third of that money, much of the remainder is reinvested into the company's growth, and some of it is used as cash flow to pay monthly bills.

And if a company is highly profitable, that's another reason to share the information. People feel secure working for a financially strong organization and are less likely to shop for other jobs. Transparency is a great practice to ensure you have top talent that stays.

SNAPSHOT OF MEETING

Participants: Everyone is invited

Frequency: Monthly

Duration: Sixty minutes

Meeting Style: Information sharing; creative discussion; consensus decision

WEEKLY ACTION REVIEW MEETINGS

THE WEEKLY ACTION REVIEW meeting, or WAR meeting, is a sixty- or ninety-minute meeting of the leadership team or a particular business area team.

The first third of the meeting involves each person on the team explaining his or her goals for the upcoming week. They go over last week's goals and address the reasons why they hit or missed them. This meeting offers an opportunity for people to talk about aspects that are going well and those that aren't. This is also the time to discuss position openings within the business area, so everyone is aware of current employees changing seats or the new people likely to take their place.

In the next third of the meeting, the team will review their numbers and discuss their key metrics. Finally, the remainder of the meeting is devoted to problem-solving for anyone facing a sticky issue. The team will likely spend the first five minutes listening to someone present his or her problem, followed by another fifteen to twenty minutes for the group to share ideas and experiences and to brainstorm ways to help troubleshoot the challenge.

This meeting helps the team to remain aligned in their objectives and goals, because everyone is made aware of what everyone else is working on and why. It might, for instance, become apparent that certain business areas need assistance from other areas of the company. The WAR meeting helps a team to foresee and get ahead of roadblocks that may arise from this situation. Someone from marketing, for example, might be working on a core project that involves finance. But someone from the finance team may say, "I can't touch this for three weeks." This information may allow marketing to defer the project for an additional week and turn its attention to another project while they wait on finance. This simply reinforces the interdependencies within the business across all areas.

WAR meetings also hold people accountable to the group. Everyone commits to his or her goals in front of everyone else. However, what is arguably most effective about WAR meetings is probably less holding others accountable, and more holding yourself accountable because you've committed to accomplishing a goal. And because everyone is working together, this instills and encourages a feeling of camaraderie, as opposed to loneliness. When everyone on the team understands that one of their own is stuck, they're able to rally around that individual and help solve the problem.

I was inspired to use the WAR meeting style for all the worldwide companies I coach because of what I witnessed at the Entrepreneur's Organization, the Young President's Organization, and Vistage. These three organizations boast as members thousands of entrepreneurs worldwide, and they all use the WAR meeting style.

One important piece of advice is to stack your meetings according to priority. You will want to have a WAR meeting among your leadership team, and this one should take place first. Then each business area should hold a WAR meeting immediately after the leadership one. For example, the leadership team could meet from 11:00 a.m. until noon to discuss their goals and remain accountable. Then immediately following that meeting, each business area could host their WAR meeting from noon to 1:00 p.m.

Stacking meetings like this allows the leaders of each business area to report back and update their teams on what happened in the leadership WAR session. After their report, the business area leader may simply listen for the rest of the meeting, without engaging too much or leading the entire WAR meeting for their area.

Ideally, each business area runs its WAR meetings simultaneously. This helps to establish a rhythm within the organization, and it allows the CEO to drop in selectively to different WAR meetings to listen and provide perspective.

SNAPSHOT OF MEETING

Participants: Leadership team or a particular business area team

Frequency: Weekly

Duration: Sixty to ninety minutes

Meeting Style: First half: information sharing; second half: creative discussion

WEEKLY STRATEGY MEETING

THE IDEA of the Weekly Strategy Meeting comes from J. D. Rockefeller. Rockefeller was a billionaire a hundred years ago. I figured that, if the guy was that smart back then, I'd incorporate what he did into my companies today. One of the things he did exceptionally well was he recognized that the team needed to have time in their calendar on a weekly and monthly basis to talk about strategy.

Strategy is a discussion of things that might go well or might go poorly in six to twelve months. These meetings typically occur every week or semi-monthly and last a couple of hours. They take place either among the leadership team or among a business area. This isn't a meeting to make decisions, but it's instead about leaning into the future to talk about what's coming and to brainstorm ideas. Typically, a running list of potential topics is kept, so the team can choose one to two topics to discuss per meeting.

An example of a Weekly Strategy Meeting might involve a discussion of the stock market's volatility. The team will ask questions such as, "What if the stock market crashes more than it has this week?" or "What if we have a 30 percent drop in the stock market? What would that do to us? What would that do to our employees? What would that do to our investments?"

This type of meeting might raise even bigger questions such as, "What if there is a war with North Korea?" or "What if something goes really well, like the product we're launching is wildly successful, and we have to rapidly scale up?" or "What if one of our biggest competitors goes bankrupt? What could we do in that event?"

Again, you don't have to end a Weekly Strategy Meeting with a resolution or put specific plans into action. The meeting is meant to be a time for the team to sit together, prognosticate the future, and throw stuff on the walls to see what sticks.

More importantly, it's about creating time for you and your team to adopt a strategic mindset within the company. You need to make time for strategy discussions and to put it on your calendar, because if you don't, then you will become reactionary. But if you make time for strategy and for brainstorming on various topics, then you will grow in a much stronger way.

SNAPSHOT OF MEETING

Participants: Leadership team; business area team

Frequency: Weekly or semi-monthly

Duration: Couple of hours

Meeting Style: Creative discussion

THE WEEKLY GOAL-SETTING AND REVIEW MEETING (ONE-ON-ONE)

WEEKLY GOAL-SETTING and review meetings, also known as the One-on-One, is a meeting between a leader and a person who directly reports to him or her. These are perhaps the most consequential meetings to take place. It's during this time that the leader sets goals with those who directly report to him or her for the upcoming week in alignment with the objectives of their team and the company.

These meetings generally happen every Monday, and

they typically last for up to sixty minutes, though sometimes for as little as thirty minutes.

While email communication is important, it's also impersonal and imprecise, and it can lead to miscommunication. In fact, 80 percent of emails between a leader and those who directly report to him or her can be eliminated during a One-on-One meeting.

In these One-on-One meetings, the leader's role is to provide a balance on three things: direction, development, and support.

Direction is making sure the person is working on the right stuff for the week. These meetings aren't about tasks or project follow-up. There are systems to track those projects, such as Asana or Basecamp. These meetings are about slowing down to communicate effectively on issues, to discuss what works and what doesn't, and generally to take stock of where things stand. They are also a chance to ensure that individuals pass along important information to those who directly report to them as well.

Development is about helping people to grow, which—as I've said before—is one of the key roles of a leader. Think about flipping the organizational chart upside down so that the CEO is at the bottom holding up the vice presidents, who hold up the managers, who holding up the customers. This meeting, in particular, gives leaders a fresh perspective on the skills of those who directly report to them. As they talk through core projects or initiatives, they might realize previously overlooked strengths and weaknesses. By identifying weaker areas, the leader can provide resources to that person or mentor him or her to build and develop a particular skill.

Support is providing the emotional buttressing, professionally and personally, to make sure the person understands that leadership cares and supports him or her individually, as well as the entire team, in good times and bad. This emotional support is especially important for people working in tough, stressful positions in high-growth environments.

When employees know this is a standing, regularly scheduled meeting locked into the leader's calendar, it provides them with a source of security and stability. It's very empowering for them to know they have their manager's ear when they need it, rather than having to fight to try to get time.

It is, therefore, important that these meetings be non-negotiable. If you're responsible for managing people, *do not* bump these meetings, even when business becomes crazy and hectic. These should be in your calendar and color coded so they don't get moved. These meetings have to happen. I consider them some of the immovable rocks in the week, so everything else is scheduled around them.

Now, if you have an employee who does the same thing week to week, you can probably get away with a thirty-minute meeting. But if the person has many different aspects of the job to deal with, then sixty minutes is more appropriate.

And bear in mind that these are in-person meetings, or over video if you're a remote team. Visual contact is necessary. In fact, I would say that it's critical. The telephone should be your absolute last resort. And in this day and age, when you have access to apps such as Zoom, there is no excuse to miss important visual cues and engagement that you can only obtain by seeing someone.

SNAPSHOT OF MEETING

Participants: Leader and one person who directly reports to him or her

Frequency: Weekly, usually on Mondays

Duration: Thirty to sixty minutes

Meeting Style: Creative discussion, consensus decision

THE DAILY HUDDLE AND ADRENALINE MEETING

THE DAILY HUDDLE

The Daily Huddle is a short, approximately seven-minute, all-company meeting designed to raise the energy level of the group and to ensure everyone is on the same page. The first couple of minutes you will spend sharing good news, before diving into the numbers, followed by the daily forecast, then the developmental update, then airtime to discuss any missing systems and frustrations, before finally wrapping it up with the cheer.

There's no sitting down during these meetings;

everyone stands up because it forces people to move and think a little faster, without the luxury of getting too comfortable. The best time of day to run these meetings is around 11:00 a.m. or 2:00 p.m., because this is when energy levels start to ebb. Part of your goal in the Daily Huddle is to boost those energy levels. You may choose to run the Daily Huddle from 10:55 a.m. to 11:02 a.m. and again from 1:55 p.m. to 2:02 p.m.

You will want to spend the first two minutes sharing good news and telling the group what is going well in the company. Maybe that means a certain business area hit a goal, a project was accomplished, someone started a new job with the company, or customers provided nice feedback. Always be hard-hitting and moving forward, full of spirit. This really raises the energy level of the group.

The next aspect of the meeting involves looking at the numbers. This is an opportunity to report the numbers that the team is hitting in real terms against the goal metrics. Again, this rallies the troops and keeps the energy high. After sharing the numbers, it's important to explain what they mean. I like to put those numbers in perspective by measuring them against our quarterly and annual goals.

After that, one area of the business should provide an update. I tend to list all of the business areas in the company and then cycle through them over the course of one to two weeks. One day, marketing will give its updates, and the next time is the finance team's turn, then IT, and so on through each business area. This gives everyone a chance to hear, learn from, and take the pulse of other business areas.

Every update is done the same way, and each business area answers the same questions:

- What are you working on?
- What were you working on last week?
- What are you stuck on?
- Is there anybody that you're hiring?

The next phase involves the team sharing any missing systems and venting their frustrations. This is a time for people to speak up about an area that's apparently broken or where they're stuck. Bear in mind, this is not the venue to solve the problem. This is the space for people to address the problems they face.

When someone shares a frustration, then someone else raises their hand and says, "I will take it," meaning they will take ownership and see to it the problem gets fixed. Later that day, week, or month, that person will come back to the group and report on the issue to explain how it was addressed and handled. This is a no-blame environment. In a growing company, stuff happens, and it's up to the team to fix and address it as it goes.

At last, the seven-minute meeting finishes with a high-gloss cheer based on something that was born out of the good news shared at the start of the meeting. I know, it's a bit hokey, but it really does work. This is similar to the breaking of a football huddle, where the players throw their hands into the center of the group and yell, "Ready, break!" It's a positive way to send people back to their desks. Admittedly, at first the Daily Huddle may feel dorky and awkward. It did when I ran 1-800-GOTJUNK?, but your people will grow to love it. In fact, at 1-800-GOTJUNK?, it's still used today.

If you want to check out an example of a seven-minute Daily Huddle, go to: youtube.com/watch?v=U1Do6tyffEo

ADRENALINE MEETING

As companies grow in size, the Daily Huddle won't work. You can't ask two hundred people to stop what they're doing and come to a meeting twice a day. That's why I created the Adrenaline Meeting to act like a Daily Huddle but on a smaller scale.

The Adrenaline Meeting is a short, three-minute meeting for a small group that can also act as a pre–Daily Huddle or a stand-alone meeting. It differs from the Daily Huddle because it's independent from the larger company. The marketing team, for instance, would run a meeting while the finance team would have its own too. But they wouldn't meet together, as they would in a Daily Huddle.

One caveat with these meetings is that the two-pizza rule doesn't apply. Go ahead and invite as many people as possible from within the business area.

IMPORTANCE OF DAILY MEETINGS

I expect everyone to show up for 100 percent of the Adrenaline Meetings or the Daily Huddles. The only time someone would ever go back to their desk is if there was an emergency or something urgent needed addressing. Everyone schedules these meetings into their calendars for the entire year, so everything else is scheduled around these times.

I used to have a company-wide alarm bell go off two minutes prior to the Daily Huddle to make sure everyone showed up exactly on time. These aren't casual meetings in which your people filter in and grab a cup of coffee or hang out around the water cooler. The huddle master, for lack of a better term, stands at the front, able to see everyone in the group and able to watch the clock, to keep track of time.

Feel free to brand these meetings in any way you like. Personalize your Daily Huddles or Adrenaline Meetings by giving them a name that helps identify them, which, in turn, helps to establish an organizational culture.

Again, meetings don't have to waste time. Even these short ones, if run properly, can align your people, restore the pulse of the office, raise energy levels, motivate, inspire, educate, unite, and provide a much-needed break in the middle of the day.

SNAPSHOT OF MEETING

Participants: Daily Huddle: everyone in the company; Adrenaline Meeting: business area teams

Frequency: Twice per day around the hours of 11:00 a.m. and 2:00 p.m

Duration: Daily Huddle: seven minutes; Adrenaline Meeting: three minutes

Meeting Style: information sharing

CHAPTER 18

AD HOC DEBRIEF MEETINGS

THE AD HOC DEBRIEF MEETING is a quick five- to ten-minute rundown by the team involved in an initial meeting, call, project, or event, and the meeting is designed to provide others in the company with the pertinent information about its execution.

The setup is very informal and only takes place on an ad hoc basis. However, don't let that mislead you. These are powerful meetings that can help a company rapidly improve its performance. Recently, I ran one with a company called Maverick Business Adventures. We held a large retreat at a summer camp for about 150 CEOs from around the world. The meeting involved going through the financials from the event and the entire P&L to discover what the revenue was supposed to be on different levels of ticket sales and sponsorships. Then, we asked ourselves how we did. We looked at every expense area we had anticipated and evaluated our execution.

The Ad Hoc Debrief Meeting provides this opportunity to go over the things that went well, the things that didn't, and how the team can learn and do better the next time.

In the case of Maverick Business Adventures, the retreat ended on a Sunday, and we held the meeting on the following Wednesday with all the stakeholders involved. It's important to keep this follow-up in relatively close proximity to the event being discussed, because it keeps ideas fresh in people's minds.

This meeting isn't complicated; it's quite simple. All you need is to ask the team questions such as these:

· What went well?
· What didn't go well?
· What can we do better next time?
· What should we continue to do next time?

SNAPSHOT OF MEETING

Participants: The team who ran a meeting, call, project, or event, plus other people

Frequency: Ad hoc

Duration: Five to ten minutes

Meeting Style: Information sharing, creative discussion, consensus decision

EVERYTHING YOU NEED TO KNOW ABOUT VIRTUAL MEETINGS

VIRTUAL MEETINGS have increased in frequency more than in-person, face-to-face ones, and that's a trend set to continue in the coming years. But the basic tenets used to conduct an in-person meeting remain the same in the virtual sphere.

Video conferencing tools such as Zoom, Google Hangout, or Skype make it possible for you to see everyone on the same call simultaneously. The visual aspect is powerful and important. Without the visual, too many distractions can tempt people when they're not engaged through eye contact. So, if you're going to hold a virtual meeting, video technology is the ideal way to go.

Video conferencing also gives you the option to use other vital tools during a meeting. Something as simple as Google Docs allows multiple users to work simultaneously on a document. Instead of emailing or faxing a document back and forth and trying to highlight changes, participants on the call can update documents in real time, adding their notes and comments. There's also virtual whiteboard software, and other software that allows you to put sticky notes up on a virtual wall to then move around.

The key is to leverage technology to the greatest extent possible in a way that makes the virtual meeting as effective and efficient as an offline one. And with technology today, that's entirely possible.

Many people ask what they can do to make virtual meetings run smoothly. I've found that just being conscious of the obvious shortcomings of the technology goes a long way. If you're on an UberConference call without video chat, remember the person on the other end can't see you, so they don't know when you want to chime in. The best thing you can do is to leave pauses in your speech to allow someone to jump in, whether that's to ask a question, add a point, or just explain that something was inaudible.

People, some more than others, often rely a lot on nonverbal communication. Think about the way we acknowledge what someone is saying with a nod or a hand gesture. If someone on the other end of the line who has spoken for five solid minutes hears only silence on your end, at some point they might ask if you're still there. Making the occasional small noise goes a long way for the person on the other end to know you're still alive and listening to them.

I've coached many CEOs from around the world whom I've never met in person. But after coaching them for years, I know all about them—their mannerisms, gestures, whether they're having a good day or bad—because that's the power of video and audio technology today.

All the different types of meetings I've covered in the previous chapters can work in a virtual setting, with the exception of the Daily Huddle and Adrenaline Meetings. That's not to say you can't hold those over video conferencing or a phone call. It will work, just not as effectively. It becomes a little bit harder, for instance, to share good news. But in fact, I have known companies that have literally phoned in their

Daily Huddles for years.

I have a friend who owns an advertising company in Nashville, Tennessee. No matter where in the world he is, he phones into his team's Daily Huddle, as does anyone else on the team who works remotely. It works for them.

In the end, there's no reason why your virtual meetings can't be as successful as your in-person ones.

MEETINGS THAT DON'T SUCK

I'VE COVERED A LOT of different meetings in this book and how to run them effectively, productively, and properly. If you are reading this book and are just coming into the workforce, you might think you will be in meetings all the time. The truth is, it's not nearly as bad as you think.

Meetings actually account for a small fraction of your time, about 20 percent. Yes, that's still a lot of time, but the good news is we can drastically reduce that number with some simple actions outlined in this book. First, we can attempt to cut the time we think we need in half. Then we can cut that time down further by allowing people who should opt out of attending a meeting to do so. We can still reduce that time even more by controlling the idle chatter and appointing a moderator and other key roles to keep meetings and attendees in check.

We may still attend as many meetings as before, but they will run more streamlined and smoothly. And who knows, maybe we will attend more meetings for the very reason that no time is wasted at them.

That's the power of running a meeting properly. You save time, money, and resources for yourself and those around you. You may also notice that the number of emails cluttering your inbox go down, the amount of miscommunication lowers, and overall employee frustration is reduced.

Properly run meetings help build your team, your culture, and your organization. As a result, you will get more done, more quickly, and with fewer people. And now that you're aware of these skills, you can share them with your leadership team and teach them to those who directly report to you.

The tools laid out in this book are to meetings what throwing, catching, and hitting are to baseball; they are the basic fundamentals that allow you to excel at—to win—the game. If you follow the principles to running a meeting, then like a great, thrilling game of baseball, you may also find that you have a lot of fun.

At the very least, your meetings will no longer suck.

ABOUT THE AUTHOR

CAMERON HEROLD has taken twenty years of experience operating some of the biggest business success stories in North America and turned it into a flourishing career as both a business consultant and a motivational speaker. Cameron is a business coach and mentor to several fast-growth businesses and a CEO coach to large corporations throughout Canada and the United States.

"Book In A Box was an incredible experience. All I had to do was talk about what I know, they did the rest, and the book is exactly what I wanted it to be."

—CAMERON HEROLD

IT'S TIME TO WRITE YOUR BOOK

Cameron spent the first half of his life building and scaling companies, and he was very good at that. He decided to spend the second half of his life helping other people achieve their dreams, and dedicated himself to teaching what he learned to entrepreneurs and CEOs.

What he didn't want to do was spend that time slaving away at a keyboard. He knew he had multiple books in him, but he couldn't find the time to sit down, type them out, and go through the whole publishing process.

So, just like when he was a CEO or COO and had to find innovative solutions to hard problems, he solved his book problem by working smarter, not harder. He used us.

Book In A Box is a company that turns ideas into books.

We surround our authors with a team of publishing professionals that help clarify and structure their book idea, get their words out of their head (in their voice), and then professionally publish their book, in about 10x less time than if they do it themselves.

Cameron used us for the book you have in your hands (and his two other recent books). And he liked us so much, he came onboard as an advisor (we're learning the same business lessons from him and his books that you are as we grow our company).

If you have valuable ideas in your head as well, and believe they might make a good book, we're happy to talk and see if we can help.

Start here: **www.bookinabox.com/CameronHerold**